REDIRECTION

By

Cynthia McInnis

Redirection
ISBN-13: 978-0-9679516-9-0
ISBN-10: 0-9679516-9-0

Copyright ©2019 by Cynthia McInnis

Published by
BALM2 Productions, Inc.
Brooklyn, NY

Printed in the United States of America.
This book or parts thereof may not be reproduced in any form, stored in a retrieval system, or transmitted in any form by any means – electronic, mechanical, photocopy, recording or otherwise- without prior written permission of the publisher, except as provided by the United States of America copyright law.

This book is available at special quantity discounts for bulk purchase for sales promotions, fund-raising and educational needs. For information please write fulleffectmail@aol.com.

DEDICATION

To those of us who fought through the temptation to prove we were right. Redirection is dedicated to those of us who stretched our tightly wound emotions out of shape, to be vulnerable and transparent. Finally to those of us who fought hard for change and won.

ACKNOWLEDGMENTS

Special thanks to

My husband; my friend, my partner in life, Bishop Archie L. McInnis, II a.k.a BALM2.

My three amazing children, Chelsea Victoria Still, Archie L. McInnis, III and Aaron L. McInnis, and my awesome Son-in-law, Treva Still

My incredible mother, Mary E. Johnson and my beautiful family.

My Father and Mother n-law, Bishop Archie McInnis, Sr. and Beverly McInnis and the family

My Publisher, Editor, sister and friend, Elder Wanza Leftwich and BALM2 Productions

To the Dream Team! We get it done.

INTRODUCTION

One of the most quintessential and life-changing moments in my life began with what I immediately perceived as a degrading insult. It was the day that I found myself, once again, sitting in the *hot seat* in my pastor's office, after yet, another outburst; another incident; another fight or, at minimum, another disagreement. After a long rampage of flying thoughts and loud accusations, bursts of tears, banters of angry monologue and ferocious sarcasm, with a long pause that was, to me, a deafening silence, a final exhale, he said, "Cynthia. There is something wrong with the way you *think.*"

I was right! Everything I said made sense to me. His opinion of me was clearly one-sided and filtered by the conversations of my enemies. They had already spoken, and he had come to a conclusion about me based on what they were saying about me. It was not fair. In essence, without saying it, I was convinced that he was not fit to judge me. He didn't even have enough sense to get a fair assessment of the situation. Again! I was misunderstood.

I would no longer hear him. Instead of listening, I sat, *waiting to talk*. Waiting to prove him wrong about me. Waiting to get him to see things from my perception. My ears were open, but my heart was locked shut. My mind was stapled securely to the closed box of my perception.

It was not until later that night, after a failed meeting, that left me angrier and more frustrated than I was at its beginning, that I found myself feeling extremely sad … again. How did things manage to go from bad to worse …again? What was I thinking? I realized that I went into that room with a fierce determination to prove that I was right, and they were all wrong. I did not want to hear anything to the contrary. I thought if I just told him my truth, he would accept it as the only truth and I would be excused for my behavior. Well, that did not happen, instead I was told that there was something wrong with the way *I think*.

Although it sounded like the worse insult ever and I tried desperately not to hear it, I kept hearing it over and over. It would ultimately change my life.

Redirection is a book that offers its reader an opportunity to look again! I want to give you a reason to consider seeing things through other perceptions in order to achieve successful outcomes in every area of your life.

Your purchase is your agreement to give me that chance. If, after reading this book, you are not seeing any successful changes in your life, you will have challenged me to write another book, a better book with your outcomes at heart.

Enjoy and be blessed,
LadyDocta

Table of Contents

PERCEPTION 1
RELATIONSHIP 4
SPIRITUAL PERCEPTION 17
MISGUIDED PERCEPTION 25
FAMILY 43
THE ME NOBODY KNOWS 55
INTRODUCE YOURSELF 65
THE ENEMIES AROUND US 75
FIGHT YOUR FIGHT! 78
THE WHY? 88
THE BUSINESS 103

REDIRECTION

PERCEPTION

To perceive is to become aware through the senses. A relationship with God gives us an additional sense; a spiritual sense that goes beyond the natural senses of sight, hearing, touch, speech and smell.

Spiritual perception is to become aware through spiritual senses. These spiritual senses are ignited by the word of God. Using your spiritual sense is commonly referred to as having *discernment*. *"And they shall teach my people the difference between the holy and profane, and cause them to discern between the clean and the unclean."* Ezekiel 44:23

Spiritual discernment is not like osmosis or psychic energy. It is not the, *something told me not to go that way* connotation. It is more like a reverberation of something you have read in God's word or an unction of the Holy Spirit that references God's word.

Discernment is considered a gift, denoting that not everyone has it. It has to be given and it can only be given by God. The Greek word for the gift of discernment is *Diakrisis*. The word describes being able to distinguish, discern, judge or appraise a person, statement, situation, or environment. In the New Testament it describes the ability to distinguish between spirits as in 1 Corinthians 12:10, and to discern good and evil as in Hebrews 5:14.

The Holy Spirit gives the gift of discernment to enable certain Christians to clearly recognize and distinguish between the influence of God, Satan, the world and the flesh in a given situation. The church needs those with this gift to warn Believers in times of danger or keep them from being led astray by false teaching. (Excerpts from Spiritualgifttest.com Spiritual Gift of Discernment)

Admittedly, I was very tempted to write this book in such way that Unbelievers could benefit from it as well as Believers, but my spiritual senses kicked in and I was reminded of my purpose in the earth. While Unbelievers will certainly benefit from this book, it was not written for them. It was written for Believers. I understand clearly that, "... *to be carnally minded is*

REDIRECTION

death; but to be spiritually minded is life and peace. Because the carnal mind is enmity against God; for it is not subject to the law of God, neither indeed can be." Romans 8:6, 7

In order for change to happen, we need God. We need to know his word. His will is his word and his word *is* his will. If a matter is to be resolved fully it must be evidenced by the word of God. So then, this book is for mature Christians who are not biblically illiterate. It is not so much for the new convert as it is for the more seasoned Christian.

It is however, a great benefit to the carnal-minded Christian who is intent on getting better outcomes in life. It will challenge and draw them closer to God and cause them to be redirected to God's will for their lives.

Cynthia McInnis

RELATIONSHIP

PSALM 51

To the chief Musician, A Psalm of David, when Nathan, the prophet came unto him, after he had gone in to Bath-sheba

[1] Have mercy upon me, O God, according to thy lovingkindness: according unto the multitude of thy tender mercies blot out my transgressions
[2] Wash me thoroughly from mine iniquity, and cleanse me from my sin.
[3] For I acknowledge my transgressions: and my sin is ever before me.
[4] Against thee, thee only have I sinned and done this evil in thy sight: that though mightiest be justified when thou speakest, and be clear when thou judgest.
[5] Behold, I was shapen in inquity: and in sin did my mother conceive me
[6] Behold, thou desirest truth in the inward parts: and in the hidden part thou shalt make me to know wisdom.

REDIRECTION

[7] Purge me with Hyssop, and I shall be clean: wash me, and I shall be whiter than snow.
[8] Make me to hear joy and gladness; that the bones which thou hast broken may rejoice.
[9] Hide thy face from my sins, and blot out all mine iniquities.
[10] Create in me a clean heart, O God; and renew a right spirit within me.
[11] Cast me not away from thy presence; and take not thy holy spirit from me.
[12] Restore unto me the joy of thy salvation; and uphold me with thy free spirit.
[13] Then will I teach transgressors thy ways; and sinners shall be converted unto thee.

This book delves directly into the heart of sincere relationship. It focuses on the many different outcomes that occur as a direct result of proper or misguided perception. As we consider spiritual perception, we must also consider our relationship with Christ as tantamount to developing proper relationships with each other.

The words we hear in Psalm 51 are the words of a man who is broken; a man who has experienced a painful fracture in a relationship that he cherished more than anything. While David is lamenting his part in the adulterous affair and deliberate murderous agenda of a devout soldier, this psalm depicts an even greater sorrow. David is distraught because his relationship with his God has been severely impacted by his action. The God who considers him the apple of his eye must be terribly disappointed by him.

This level of sorrow and penitence can only come from a heart that once truly loved. I believe that David truly loved God and I believe he had a very real relationship with him. After all, you don't go around writing songs for and about someone with whom you are not in a relationship. Psalm 42 records an intimacy in David's relationship with God as he says, "my tears have been my meat, day and night." Only real relationships evoke that many tears. David was a man *after God's own heart* so, not only was David in relationship with God, God was in relationship with him. What a devastation to have seemingly severed such a perfect set-up!

REDIRECTION

David cries out in Psalm 42:4 *"When I remember these things, I pour out my soul in me: for I had gone with the multitude, I went with them to the house of God, with the voice of joy and praise, with a multitude that kept holyday."* It sounds to me like he is saying, *I miss you!* *"As the hart panteth after the water brooks, so panteth my soul after thee, O God."* I've been there! I remember an adage that says, "It's better to have loved and lost than never to have loved at all!" It is the memory of past love than can reignite a fire gone out. It is this kind of memory that leads to true repentance.

I remember having gone so far away from God's word and ultimately, his will, that I was literally lost. I did things to satisfy a part of me that could never be satisfied. It became a stupid cycle, but one I found myself stuck in for what seemed like an eternity. It was an exacerbated season of emptiness. My prayer life had dwindled to nothingness. I had gotten so busy being busy that I subconsciously deafened my inner ear to the cries of a soul that was longing for intimacy with her real friend.

Over time, I developed friendships but for whatever reason, I was unable to sustain a real relationship. I almost thought there was something wrong with me. I was never completely vulnerable in any relationship. I never let my guard down. I never really trusted anyone's intentions for friendship with me. In fact, as soon as things began to get *too serious,* I managed to destroy the relationship. In hindsight, I understood the self-destructive nature of my character but knew without doubt that the deeply rooted core problem was that I was out of right relationship with God. I was out of sorts, un-synced. Everything felt *temporary.*

It's easy to point the finger and blame everything and everyone for my own fracturing of a perfect relationship with God. But as David says in verse 6 of Psalm 51, *Behold, thou desirest truth in the inward parts: and in the hidden part thou shalt make me to know wisdom,* I cannot lie. While people and circumstances were influential in my decisions, I had the Holy Spirit within and therefore, the strength and power to resist any temptation.

REDIRECTION

I admit that getting back to the place in God that I could feel his presence again was much more difficult than it was to drift away. What started out as a casual drift, a simple taste and an innocent inquiry ended up being a long journey to a far-away place and it would take work to get back. But I was willing to try. I missed God. I missed his touch. I missed spending time in his presence. It was a love lost but thank God, *he restores my soul!* Oh, how I thanked God for the memories. I remembered my Pastor's voice in prayer. I remembered the peace that I felt in her presence and in her home. I remembered the presence of God in prayer. I remembered the complete satisfaction in knowing that he loved me! I remembered his promise to be married to the backslider and that he would never leave me or forsake me. I heard his voice saying, come unto me all ye that labor and are heavy laden. Sin had made me burdened and heavy laden. I felt so foolish. I felt like I had wasted so much time. I got absolutely nothing from being out of the will of God. I was never satisfied. I was never truly happy. That is my truth.

When you hear the term, *backslider* you might envision me in a club with a joint or a drink. Well, it was never like that. It was the worst kind of backsliding. I was still preaching, still attending every service, still singing in the choir, still getting all dressed up for church, still teaching but with nothing! For God's own purpose he would anoint me while I preached or sang but when it was over, it was over. I went home empty and void, so after a while, I didn't go home. I went other places and did other things trying to fill a spiritual void. How dumb is it to think you could fill a spiritual void with a natural resource? When you don't pray your spiritual senses get dull and you just do dumb things. It was in that season that the girl in the introduction showed her true colors. I had one episode after the next, one disappointment after the next. Things began to get really, really bad. I lost great jobs; my brilliant mind had gotten me into more criminal activity than it could handle and I suffered much loss and knew exactly why. My ex wanted me back and I wanted him too!

REDIRECTION

My story ends well! June 27, 1998 was the day that we launched Full Effect Gospel Ministries in the basement of our home. While I would greatly miss my former church and my former pastor, I knew that this was my chance to start over! It was definitely not easy. I remember getting down on my knees to pray. In ten minutes flat, the pain that went through my then 35 year old knees was shockingly excruciating. The lack of focus and the inability to concentrate in prayer was embarrassing. Fifteen minutes in prayer felt like an hour. I was far from home but determined. It was my fault. I prayed and prayed and one day I got a breakthrough. His presence enveloped my soul. The glory of his presence had returned to my soul and like Peter, I was like, *let's build a tabernacle* right here and never leave!!!

I can hear some of you saying, it didn't take all of that. All you had to do was believe. Blah, blah, blah. That is like telling me how to make *my* marriage relationship work with your methods! What works for your relationship may not work for mine. If that is you, all I can say is, you work your relationship with God the way you work yours and I will work mine the way I work mine. I had to *press in* to his presence. I had to do spiritual warfare because my enemy didn't want me to get there. Once I experienced breakthrough, I made a holy vow that I would never let that happen again. I have since been in some dark places, and some short-lived faith challenges but I knew enough not to stay there and not to get caught out there again. I took advantage of David's Psalm 51 experience and cried out to God in truth and he restored my soul every time! Oh, how I love Jesus!

    I can almost imagine the intense internal pain Adam and Eve experienced when they expected to hear the footsteps of God coming to visit with them in the garden; I can almost feel them longing for his presence again only to find that he was not coming! The punishment he doled out to them was tolerable and well deserved. They could handle that, but this absence was the worst! I am sure they remembered a relationship that was naked and not ashamed. Can you imagine how close you are in relationship when you don't mind being naked in front of someone? No shame! I am who I am, and you accept me that way. I do not have to hide from you

REDIRECTION

because we are in a good relationship. Now they were covering themselves with leaves. God still loved them and would still provide their needs but what they longed for most was time with him.

Every Believer desires to spend time with God. God also desires to spend time with his people. Not just busy time, but quality time in prayer and worship. We must not let anything cause a breach in our relationship with God. Our time with him should never be compromised. Just as in a natural relationship, we must *make* time for unmitigated, uninterrupted, unscripted worship!

Spending time in his presence has helped to make all of my relationships better and more lasting. It is his magnificent and glorious presence that provides an audience for revelation! It is where great books, songs and sermons are birthed. Redirection in relationships will become repeated cycles if we do not first make certain that our relationships are right with God. Before going further, perhaps someone needs to pray. Perhaps you have never had the kind of intimacy and personal relationship with Christ that I am referring to. I will not take for granted that everyone reading this book enjoys a real relationship with God. I will assume that you have accepted Christ in your life and that you are born again but have you gone further than that? Have you invited Christ into your life as Lord? Do you acknowledge him in everything? Is he a recurring thought in your heart and mind? Do you ever long for his presence? Do you *need* him? Is he first in your life? I urge you to think before you answer. First, means first. Is he more important to you than your, children, your spouse, yourself? Do you cry in his presence? Does your secret sin feel like an offence to someone you love? Does violating him, violate you? Is all of this overwhelming you? Are you offended by the questions?

    The answers to the questions above merely scratch the surface. The sad truth is that many Christians live and die without having experienced the glory of a real and personal relationship with Jesus Christ. For them it is all about rules and regulations, daily penances and lists of good deeds done to others and for Christ. He has never made them smile. Just being with him has never been their satisfying moments. They lived their

REDIRECTION

entire lives wanting more. They have never truly been able to say, *I am happy with Jesus alone.* They lived and died without feeling the power of his presence. They have never been taken under by the power of his love. His presence has never filled their souls to the point that it was overflowing. It's almost like being married for years but have never been held or kissed. Living life following rules but never knowing what it feels like to be lost in the love of someone else's love. It is like loving but not being in love; so in love that you'd do almost anything just to be in the presence of your friend. A friend who you would sit with for an hour just watching them text on the phone, stare at a TV or just chew; you just want to be in the same room with that person. I know that feeling both naturally and spiritually. When Archie holds me, I feel his love going through my entire body. There is nothing better than that …except when I feel the presence of my Jesus.

    I have got to tell you how I rush to my bedroom to put on my prayer music and fall on my knees to meet him! How I close my office door and fall on the floor in worship and how I cannot wait for Tuesday and

Thursday night Prayer and Worship services! Where it once took me hours to press in to his presence, I now feel like he's already there waiting for me! One, "Oh Glory!" and it's on and poppin! Just like with Archie, it has not always been like this. Our relationship has been fractured and tried but God has restored it. Hallelujah! He restores my soul!

Before you finish reading this book, I want you to pray for a longing. Flirt with the idea of a real relationship with Jesus. Press in to his presence. If you had it and it feels lost or fractured, know that it is never gone! He promised that he would never leave you and he always keeps his promises. He is waiting for you in the place that you left him or the place that you lost your way. You can find that place in prayer and worship. Selah.

REDIRECTION

SPIRITUAL PERCEPTION

I cannot stress how very important it is to know Jesus! I mean, to know him personally; as your personal savior. As new converts, our minds have to be redirected from ideas that we have heard about Him over time. We cannot rely on another person's description of him to determine what we know about him. It has to be both biblical and personal.

We know him through His word and through our personal time spent with him. We must be redirected from adages like, *the man upstairs, the higher power or the big guy in the sky.* We'll leave those terms to those who simply acknowledge his existence but clearly do not know him personally.

Many world views argue whether a personal relationship with God is at all possible. They clearly denounce that God could possibly be a person. A ball of energy maybe, but certainly not a person; therefore, render any personalized relationship unattainable.

Matt Slick, President and Founder of the Christian Apologetics and Research Ministry says this, "We would first have to define what "person" means before we can determine if God is a person. Some people think that a person must have a body of flesh and bones, but theologically speaking "personhood" does not necessitate that. Instead, personhood is defined as having a will, self-awareness, emotions, being able to recognize others, speaking, etc. Therefore, angels would be persons since they have wills, speak, etc. God would be a person too. However, the Christian doctrine of God is that he is comprised of three persons: The Father, the Son, and the Holy Spirit. We call this the Trinity. We say that God is three persons because we see that the Father is called God (Phil. 1:2), the Son is called God (Heb. 1:8), and the Holy Spirit is called God (Acts 5:1-4). Each has a will (F, Luke 22:42; S, Luke 22:42; HS, 1 Cor. 12:11) and speaks (F, Matt. 3:17; S, Luke 5:20; HS, Acts 13:2).

However, we do find that in the Bible "God" also speaks in the singular. For example,

REDIRECTION

- Gen. 1:29, *"And God said, 'Behold, I have given you every herb bearing seed, which is upon the face of all the earth...'"*
- Exodus 3:14, *"And God said unto Moses, 'I AM THAT I AM': and he said, 'Thus shalt thou say unto the children of Israel, I AM hath sent me unto you.'"*

This is not a contradiction between God being expressed as one person and being a Trinity of persons. The totality of the Godhead as a Trinity can certainly speak as one. So, can God be said to be a person? Yes. And how do we tell if he is a person? We simply look at the requirements of being a person, such as speaking, being aware of others, having a will, loving, etc., and we see that God most certainly expresses the attributes of personhood."

Jesus is the embodiment of God. He came to earth as a person. He was born, lived and died as both God and man. He is presently our risen savior. He left a transcript of his life because he wants to form personal relationships with man. He said, and still says, *"Come unto me ..."*

Sadly, many professed Christians are still living devoid of such a personal relationship. Somehow or another we have been distracted or turned away from the true essence of relationship with Christ and have become inundated with the doctrine and the idea of Christianity.

I once saw a movie about a woman who became so completely immersed in her passion to teach that she completely neglected her husband for her students. She became so preoccupied with their lives that she did not even see her relationship with her husband crumbling. She did not see his emptiness. She did not see his loneliness. She simply ignored his words and eventually, she no longer saw him at all. When challenged with the "why" of his request for a divorce, after saying, "I love being married to you, why would you do this?" His answer was, "You love the *idea* of marriage."

Too many Christians are in love with the concept of Christianity but no longer see the Christ of Christianity. They must be redirected! Those Christians must be led back to the person of Jesus Christ and form personal relationships with him.

REDIRECTION

It is not until a true relationship with Christ is formed that we understand the power of that relationship. Like in any relationship, time is tantamount. Just as Christ came as a seed in the womb of a virgin, so our relationship with him must begin with a seed. The seed of his word must be planted in our hearts. It must be nourished and protected so that we can see it growing.

I said earlier that this book is not so much for the new convert but for the more seasoned Christian knowing full well that it is often very difficult to tell the difference between the two. My desire is that a Christian reading this book who considers himself seasoned simply because he has professed to be a Christian for many years would be redirected. Redirected to the place of that new convert who, like a baby, knows that he needs everything from Christ to survive. The babe in Christ who desires the sincere milk of the Gospel. *"As new born babes, desire the sincere milk of the word, that ye may grow thereby"* 1 Peter 2:2KJV

This book also comes to the truly seasoned Christian that may have become so involved in the activities, doctrines or concepts of Christianity that they have allowed their personal relationship with him to dwindle. Let me redirect you to what really matters in life.

For those who are so concerned with *the body beautiful* and spend more time correcting it than they do with building and maintaining a personal relationship with Christ, 2 Corinthians 5:1 KJV reminds us of this, *"For we know that if our earthly house of this tabernacle were dissolved, we have a building of God, an house not made with hands, eternal in the heavens."*

Am I telling you to forget about your health, ignore your physical flaws, don't comb your hair or clean your house? Of course not! But redirect the attention paid to it with God's word in your heart and mind. This way, if something devastating or irreparable should happen to this body we have an assurance that only our relationship with Christ can provide.

Remember, spiritual discernment is an unction from the Holy Spirit that coincides with God's word. You will get, what the older saints would call, *"a knowing in your knower"* that everything is going to be alright.

REDIRECTION

Baby Christians spend more time getting dressed for church than the service actually takes. I want to redirect the focus of so many church going Christians from fashion to faith. When church looks like an all-out fashion show, it's just too much. People are not focused correctly and too much emphasis is being placed on self. "Look at me. See me. Value me. Love me" screams louder than praise.

I want to help redirect people to our original design so that we will have no need to starve for attention and draw the focus away from the cross. *"I will praise thee; for I am fearfully and wonderfully made: marvelous are thy works; and that my soul knoweth right well."* Psalms 139:14

It is this redirection to right relationship with Christ that will urge right relationships with others. One relationship will effectively dictate to the other. Who we date, who we marry and how we relate to one another will all come from the same place.

The most important part of redirection is the emphasis on personal relationship with Christ. This book is an attempt to show how we can have better outcomes by changing our perceptions. We must immerse ourselves in the study of God's word to develop spiritual perceptions. We must pray for the gift of discernment.

REDIRECTION

MISGUIDED PERCEPTION

I have chosen to throw myself under the bus in this work as a sacrifice for the betterment of others. Thank me later. When I got married nearly 28 years ago, I never said it or even thought of it, but I learned later that I really wanted to be the perfect wife. I just wanted to do everything right. As you have probably learned from reading about the girl in the introduction, not being right was a big problem for me. Needless for me to say, I was wrong ... a lot. In this chapter I will share some of the misguided perceptions I had as a wife. (God help me!)

First of all, it was misguided to think I could be the perfect wife with no training, no experience and no personal mentors. It was also misguided for me to think that my new husband expected me to be the perfect wife, although it felt that way after every mistake I made.

Day after day I found myself trying to prove one thing or the other. I didn't know then that I was trying to prove things, but I found out later. I would break into fits of anger when I believed I was falsely accused. I did not use any spiritual discernment. In my mind, my marriage was not Kingdom it was just my marriage and I had to make it work. Big mistake!

Christian marriage is called Holy Matrimony; it is done in a church and sanctioned by a minister. When asked, "What should be different about a Christian Marriage?" Gotquestions.org says this, "The primary difference between a Christian marriage and a non-Christian marriage is that Christ is the center of the marriage. When two people are united in Christ, their goal is to grow in Christlikeness throughout the life of the marriage. Non-Christians may have goals for their marriage, but *Christlikeness* is not one of them. This is not to say that all Christians, when they marry, immediately begin to work toward this goal. Many young Christians don't even realize this is actually the goal, but the presence of the Holy Spirit within each of them works with them, maturing each one so that the goal of Christlikeness becomes increasingly clear to them."

REDIRECTION

Our case was very similar except we were both pretty seasoned Christians; we were both filled with the Holy Spirit and we were both well versed in the Scripture. You would think we would never, ever have a fight. Not!

Neither of us thought of the goal of our marriage as growing in Christlikeness throughout the life of the marriage. We had a misguided perception about the main goal. We knew we would both love God and serve God, but we were not using our marriage to do that.

We made spiritual plans to serve in ministry together, to love each other, to have a family, to work together financially, to establish a home and perhaps a business. We assumed that we were already Christlike and, for the most part, we were but there is nothing like marriage to show you where you are not!

Our first really heated argument began with us trying to determine who was more effective in the Civil Rights Movement; Martin Luther King or Malcom X. Why did I say Malcom X when Martin Luther King was a Christian and practiced non-violence? How could I, as a Christian, possibly believe that Malcom X was more effective?

Well, I cannot even remember what my reasons were then, and they do not matter much now. What matters most is that the argument was more about a challenge of my Christlikeness than my civil rights opinion. Some of our fiercest fights were challenges to each other's Christian character. Most arguments would end up with statements like, "And you're supposed to be saved!"

The misguided idea that Christians cannot make mistakes in judgment and still be Christians can cause serious harm to meaningful relationships. There are entire Christian reformations and churches that do not fellowship with one another because one is right, and the other is wrong. Redirection to the Cross of Calvary should ease the pain but that is a conversation for another day.

While I cannot speak for my husband or his thought processes around those dark seasons, I can certainly speak to mine. So many times, he would say one thing and I would hear something totally different. I

REDIRECTION

confess that I may have had misguided perceptions that caused or exacerbated serious but unnecessary fights and arguments. Thank you for asking, I will share.

When my husband expressed his dislike for something I did or said, I would jump quickly to my own defense. He would say, "I don't like *it*" but I would hear, "*I don't like you*" in hindsight, I can hear myself saying over and over, "Maybe you should go find the kind of wife you really want." My perception was that he just didn't like *me*. I responded every single time with that perception and I realize now that I was trying, for many years, to prove that I was right about that perception. It was self-destructive. It was the reason I did not have lasting relationships. I would believe that my lack of perfection caused people to dislike me and I was determined to prove it. How dumb is that? It was my reality. My misguided perception that everyone expected me to do everything right and if I didn't, they would no longer care for me was a big mistake. It was quite grand of me to think anyone even thought I could be perfect.

I worked the overnight shift at Dow Jones, Inc. and I had abused my Black-Car privilege by taking black cars to church services on my lunch break. My heart was right, but my work ethic was poor. It turned out that the company found out, of course, and my supervisor called me in. Instead of owning up to my mistake in judgment, agreeing to pay the bills in an attempt to keep a great job, I quit. I left a resignation letter under his door during the night shift. This was a terrible mistake. I perceived that he was going to fire me anyway and was too proud to be humiliated, especially being a Christian.

I found out later that he had no intention of firing me and had in fact done the same thing a time or two. He was ready to forgive all with a slap on the wrist but, like a fool, I had already quit.

The girl in the introduction thought her pastor, *"just didn't like her"* so she rebelled over, and over trying to prove her misguided perception. It is not until we have people in our lives who are determined to love us regardless to our misguided perceptions that we will have lasting relationships. It is precisely why Jesus could say on the cross, *"Father, forgive them for they know not what they do."* They are misguided in their perceptions about me, but they are worth saving.

REDIRECTION

If I had known then what I know now, I would have tried to see things from another perspective. I would have tried to *hear* better. I would have tried to understand things from a biblical perspective and not from my emotions and my feelings. If I had been as close to God as I thought I was, I am sure I would have handled things more spiritually maturely. I am grateful that God, my pastor and my husband were determined to love me regardless to my misguided perceptions. I thank God for *time*.

There are other misguided perceptions that work directly against marriages. Perceptions about infidelity, insecurity, intentions and mindsets can make or break a good marriage. This makes it more and more quintessential for Christian couples to work together in prayer and study. Holiness and righteous living make the Christian marriage complete. *"Righteousness exalteth a nation; but sin is a reproach to any people"* Proverbs 14:34

I cannot leave here without addressing the invisible elephant in the room; Competition. Couple after couple have come into the office for counseling and each with a fierce determination to prove who is the better mate. One may come in earlier or seek private consultation to paint the other in a very poor light. This is an effort to bring bias to the opinion of the counselor at the on-set. Everyone wants to be right. Everyone wants to be the one with the better judgment and everyone wants justification for their actions. Very few come into counseling with a sincere desire to *fix this*.

Oh, I know it quite well. You've met the girl in the introduction. It is not until things have reached the point of devastation that people like her yearn for a resolve. In the heat of the battle there is a fierce competition going on between the better spouse, the better Christian, the better parent and ultimately the better person. Both want the counselor to choose them but here lies the fundamental concept that is so big it cannot be seen; it is the inability to see the forest for the trees ... they chose each other! The husband has chosen the wife as the best choice for his marriage and the wife has chosen the husband as the best choice for her marriage! The counselor will never be able to choose

REDIRECTION

who is the better person when both are the best persons for each other. Got it?

The counselor's best option is to show these two how they are better together than they are apart. He must show them concepts and ways to work through any dilemma *together*. He must effectively redirect their drama to the greater good for them, *together*. When divorce is not an option for a Kingdom couple, redirection is the key! A wise counselor will allow this couple to expose both perceptions to each other and then offer another, more beneficial, more provable perception and that will have to come from the wisdom of God.

For example, a couple who is having a major fall-out about a co-parenting issue may bring out all of the faults perceived about each other without once addressing it from the child or children's perception. What is this doing to the child? Once this couple is able to see this situation from another perception then there is hope for a resolve. How can we work together to resolve this dilemma with the best outcomes for *all* involved? A wise counselor will be able to help here.

King Solomon faced a more devastating but similar dilemma. In 1 Kings 3:16–28 we find an account of King Solomon hearing a case involving two prostitutes. The two women had both recently given birth to sons, and they lived together in the same home. During the night, one of the infants was smothered and died. The woman whose son had died switched her dead baby with the baby of the other woman as she slept. The other woman, seeking justice, took the matter before the king. She stated her case: "We were alone; there was no one in the house but the two of us. During the night this woman's son died because she lay on him. So, she got up in the middle of the night and took my son from my side while I, your servant, was asleep. She put him by her breast and put her dead son by my breast. The next morning, I got up to nurse my son—and he was dead! But when I looked at him closely in the morning light, I saw that it wasn't the son I had borne" (verses 18–21).

Solomon could not tell from their words which woman was telling the truth. Instead, he issued a shocking command: *"Bring me a sword. . . . Cut the living child in two and give half to one and half to the*

REDIRECTION

other" (1 Kings 3:24–25). After he said this, the woman whose son was still alive said, "Please, my lord, give her the living baby! Don't kill him!" however, the other woman, whose son had died, answered, "Neither I nor you shall have him. Cut him in two!" (verse 26). Based on their responses, Solomon knew the identity of the true mother: "Give the living baby to the first woman. Do not kill him; she is his mother" (verse 27).

Why would Solomon give such an outrageous command? Did he really intend to cut a baby in half with a sword? The text is clear that Solomon's intention was to discover the truth. He did so by watching the responses of the two women and relying on the maternal instincts of the true mother. (https://www.gotquestions.org/Solomon-two-prostitutes.html)

King Solomon used the wisdom of God to redirect the mothers' thinking from themselves to the life of the child. His suggestion to cut the child in half changed their perceptions about the situation. As long as the child was alive the liar would continue to lie but the concept of a dead child brought out the truth. The wisdom of God can challenge stubborn perceptions and get down to the truth. It is not until we deal in truth, absolute truth that we can get a lasting resolve and a better outcome.

What about a couple whose marriage has simply lost its luster? The light has gone out in both of their eyes for each other. It's over. A wise counselor must redirect them back to the days when there was luster and when the lights were burning brightly and then walk them patiently through the events that happened since then. I guarantee you that somewhere along that walk they will run into a misguided perception. One that screams, "I did not think that!" "I never said that!" "I did not mean that" or "It was not like that".

Again, I will put myself out there. Thank me later. One of the most trying seasons of my marriage, when I actually took a trip down south to "breathe" was entangled by a totally misguided perception. I was always on the defense about not being wanted. So much so that not being wanted was one of two things I considered to be grounds for divorce! I would not be in a marriage where I was unwanted or unloved. I would

REDIRECTION

not try to make anyone *want* me. I was always on the lookout for it and most of my rages ended in, "Well, go and get the kind of woman you really want!" I told you earlier that when he said or showed that he did not like some*thing* I did or said, I took it to mean that he didn't like me. It is self-destructive in its nature. A self-fulfilling prophecy. I thought it, I knew it and I was determined to be right about it. I was preparing myself for an ultimate, inevitable break up that was completely unfounded. It was a misguided perception but if I continued in that vein and continued to respond to my own emotional perceptions, our marriage would not have stood a chance. This is the reason I am transparently sharing with you at the risk of you calling me all kinds of names.

I remember coming back and trying to explain to my husband that I did not feel his love for me; I did not see love in his eyes when he looked at me; I saw only disgust. The only conversations we had were complaints about one thing or another; what the members said about me, what he said about me and what I just did not do right. Perhaps we had gotten so busy being busy that what we once had was faded away and this was what we were left with. Oh, yes! My argument was real. I was emotionally distraught. I could not see anything else. I went on and on only to see in the eyes of my husband a total confusion. He had no idea where all of that was coming from. Thank God he was wise enough not to dismiss it as nothingness or female drama. I think he knew that I really believed what I was saying and was ready to do something about it. He put his arms tightly around me and squeezed me. He reassured me that he loved me very much and that he was very much in love with me. He told me that I was the best thing in his world and that he could not imagine life without me.

While this was reassuring and may have some of you shedding tears, the truth is that it had *never* ceased to be truth. He had always felt that way. It never changed but my perception of it had changed. Circumstances, times, events and misguided perceptions caused a truth to be distorted and even dismissed as non-existent.

It is true that maybe he had not said it enough. It's true that maybe we had gotten so involved in ministry that the demands on our time together had been

REDIRECTION

a challenge. It's true that maybe I had become jealous of his time spent with the ministry and the people in the ministry. It's true that I may have been threatened by his time with others as better times than spent with me. It's true that taking care of the children, the house and the family brought some distance over time and all of this created a misguided perception of his true feelings for me.

I can hear some of you who know me thinking right now, as confident as she seems, I didn't know she was so insecure. It's O.K., neither did I. But I have learned that insecurity and vulnerability are not always bad words. I did not have anything to prove to anybody. If I had been strong enough to admit to those emotions instead of making wild unfounded assumptions, I would have had less drama in my life.

Can I help you? If I had been strong enough to say, "Baby I really want you to stay here with me tonight. I'm lonely. I'm feeling really vulnerable and insecure right now. I need my man. I need to be held ..." (I'm sure you're getting it) Instead of saying, "Are you going out again? The kids are going to say they only see me in this family because you're gone all the time ... blah, blah blah" things would probably have been a lot better for us.

On one of my re-reads, I heard in my spirit, someone asking, what if this was not the case? What if I was openly vulnerable and expressed my fears, insecurities, challenges and suspicions verbally and my spouse retorted unfavorably? What if that approach did not work? What if things got worse as a result of my vulnerability?

My answer to the voice in my spirit is ... truth. You must get to the real truth about where your relationship is and where both of you think it is going. You cannot fool yourself into believing something that is not truth and he cannot respond to you in untruthfulness. The real question is do you still love each other and are you willing to work to bring back the luster of your marriage? Once we get a truthful yes from the two of you, then we can back track to find out what really went wrong and how we can begin the healing process. What will not work is a response that says, "I do not know if I am still in love and I do not know if I am willing to work

REDIRECTION

at a resolve." That, in my opinion, is a cop-out and usually means, "No, no, and no!" Before you jump all over my head, hear this. The sentence is quite different when said this way, "At this juncture, the way I am feeling right now, I'm not sure if I still love this person or if I want to work at a resolve." Agreed? This gives the counselor some leverage and gives the couple the benefit of time and counseling, time and prayer, time and wisdom and time in truthful communication.

My stance has always been, if you're staying, I will help you stay but if you're leaving, I will help you leave, but you cannot be staying and leaving at the same time. Once a person has made up his or her mind to leave, he or she is already gone but once a person has made up his or her mind to stay, he or she may never leave. My book. My opinion. Let's stay friends.

In relationships, maturity factors play a key part. Immature people often say what they do not mean, have things to prove, play too much but eventually get to their truth. Great counselors do not spend too much time on unstable relationships, so, they will get some initial information about the couple and their relationship. The idea that most people do not seek counseling until things have completely spiraled out of order is a good thing because at least the counselor knows they're ready for change.

You may be reading this book while facing a major challenge in your relationship. I trust that it helps you begin the process of redirection! Changing perceptions for better outcomes. I pray that you become vulnerable enough to ask the right questions and strong enough to accept truthful answers. I pray that each reader takes a personal stance at redirection and not expect change from anyone else but themselves. Stay with me as we journey into other areas of redirection.

REDIRECTION

FAMILY

Wow. As I sit here beginning this chapter, I must admit that a strong reluctance has come over me. The idea of family is a very sensitive one for me as I am certain is may be for others. I believe that the strong reluctance I feel is because this chapter will be very liberating and life changing for someone, so, here I go.

I will not delve into the dynamics of family from a traditional perspective, but I will go into some unchartered areas. I will start with the untraditional foster or adoptive family concept but mainly from the perception of the person who, despite the welcoming or love they received, still feels unwanted, unloved or insignificant.

Let's rule-out the obvious Cinderella story! It is an unfortunate truth that some people become foster parents to get money. There. I said it. People like that run a dangerous risk of ruining the lives they are entrusted to save. I submit that there are much better ways to make money than on the emotional vulnerability of children! Get a real life.

While we cannot take away the foolishness of the world, we can focus our hearts on the genuine and sincere in heart. That parent, that caregiver who has given his or her all at trying to love and cover a child given to them by God or any other means only to be constantly challenged by accusations and painful insults to the exact opposite.

A child, who should be quick to forgive all perceived wrong-doings of a parent on the premise of unconditional love, spews countless painful words in the face of the caregiver. This must be indescribably difficult to comprehend. How can they not see my love? How can they not feel my heart? How can they not know my true desires for them? These are some of many questions that disturb the sleep of a loving caregiver.

The answers all lie under the cover of individual perception. There is a reason that this child seemingly cannot see, feel or know. This is what we have to get to. They are all the right questions, but we need guidance from God, spiritual discernment to get to those answers.

REDIRECTION

It will take a deliberate selflessness to get to the undercurrent of this child's truth. This caregiver must, in essence, give himself away to the mindset of the child and place himself in his shoes, completely from his perspective.

This will be very difficult, because if the parent bought the bedroom set, pays the mortgage and bought the toilet tissue, they will see this child an ungrateful, spoiled brat. They will see the bedroom as a privilege, the heat in the home as a blessing and the toilet tissue as a personal courtesy! How dare this so and so be unhappy?

Now, let's take this situation a step further. A husband that pays the bills, provides all for the family and the wife; works hard to provide the best for his family only to come home and see a sadness in his wife's eyes or to hear complaints about this or that from the children; he could really care less what all that sadness is about. From his perspective, they should all be grateful and stop whining.

The parent and the husband could take this approach and leave it at that or they can redirect their thinking to another perspective to get a better outcome. I get it. It's much easier to see these people as ingrates and say it is what it is, become the victim and walk it out but we all know how that will end. To say the least, frustration is inevitable.

Alex Lickerman, M.D., in an article in *Psychology Today,* writes about dealing with frustration in close relationships (which is maybe even more pronounced during this busy time of year). "It's an uncomfortable paradox that the people closest to us often frustrate us the most. My theory about this is that we all have a certain level of tolerance for frustration that diminishes with repeated exposure to a situation or a person we find frustrating. Thus we more easily manage our frustration at the beginning of a frustrating experience and with people we've only just met, but as time passes and our frustration continues, our ability to manage it steadily decreases... Our closest family members populate the most intimate areas of our lives and often limit our ability to find privacy or refuge in which to rest and thereby temporarily regain an ability to tolerate things that (and people who) frustrate us...

REDIRECTION

Poorly managed frustration is toxic to relationships. It causes a build-up of resentment that—even when over only small things—can ultimately overwhelm any desire to relate in a positive fashion. And no one likes living in a perpetual state of annoyance or anger (no matter how much it may seem like they do)...

Trying to suppress or ignore frustration seems only to make it worse; often causing us to magnify the import of whatever complaint we have against whomever frustrated us...Instead of willpower, then, the best antidote upon which I've stumbled involves the use of gratitude. Now when I become frustrated, I strive to immediately remind myself of all the things I *appreciate* about the person who's frustrated me. Undoubtedly, appreciating people we see in our day-to-day lives is the most difficult, as they're the very people not only most likely to frustrate us but also with whom we're most likely unable to control our frustration—but such people wouldn't likely be in our lives so consistently in the first place if they didn't have important qualities that we valued. Reminding ourselves of those qualities shouldn't, therefore, be too difficult."

When it comes to children and spouses, we all know that there is an expected sense of unconditional love involved but stubbornness and rigidity can cause that love to be trampled upon and disregarded. It can, in essence, become so hardened by anger, frustration and disappointment that it almost seems non-existent that is why time is a variable of great importance. We cannot afford to harbor this level of pain. We must find a way to resolve these issues through redirection.

Someone has to give themselves away! Someone has to see the other person's discomfort, not as a fault but as a dilemma. Someone must not take the other person's dilemma to blame. If it takes help, get it. If it takes prayer, do it. If it takes time, spend it. This person must mean more to you than your own personal feelings. *Let nothing be done through strife or vainglory; but in lowliness of mind let each esteem other better than themselves.* Philippians 2:3

When my husband expressed, over and over, that he felt disrespected by me, I continued to rebuttal that he

REDIRECTION

was in fact, not disrespected. After all, I should know if I respected him or not. This went on for many years. From my perspective I respected him greatly. I honored his work ethic, I honored his spiritual posture, I honored his gallant fatherhood and his unselfish espousal, in fact, I thought he was the absolute man!

It was not until he said something right in the midst of a heated argument that I finally got a revelation. I was strongly debating my position (for the sake of decency) I guess he would say I was loud, obnoxious and disrespectful and he asked me, "Would you speak this way to your boss?" I realized at that very moment that under no circumstances would I ever speak to my boss the way I was speaking to him. He said, "Cynthia, that is because of how you see him. You see him as your authority, but you see me as your equal. This is what I call disrespect." I finally got it. To him, respect was not just a feeling, it was an action. When you respect someone, you govern your emotions and your behaviors in his honor. There are just some things you do not do, some distances you just do not go, right or wrong, out of respect. He was saying this all the time but I did not hear it. I heard, "you don't" when I just knew I did.

Let's get back to parenting. I will share another very sensitive situation. By the time my daughter was in middle school we had two more children, a house with a mortgage, a new church, personal ministry engagements, while both of us were working full time jobs. Needless to say, our life was very full. We tried hard to make sure our children were well and taken care of amidst all that we had undertaken while trying to keep our marriage alive.

I noticed that my daughter seemed sad often but by then she had developed a nick-name, *"Drama Mama"*. I guess I started that because from my perspective she was just a little drama queen because nothing could possibly be going wrong with her. Compared to my life at her age, she had it made. Her constant bouts with her brothers was merely sibling rivalry and was not to be taken seriously.

She had severe Eczema but in my eyes she was my perfect princess and I looked beyond the skin discoloration, the scaly peeling skin on her hands, legs

REDIRECTION

and face. I bought cream after cream but never ever saw her as anything other than beautiful. Shoot me for being naive or stupid or slow but it never dawned on me that she was sad or angry because she was being greatly teased at school. She never told me but in hind-sight I should have perceived that. I only saw her from my own perspective. I bought her dresses that I thought were beautiful and accused her of being ungrateful when she cried about wearing them. She said the fabric was itchy, I said she just didn't like it because I picked it. I know, I know but it was what it was. I was treating the Eczema and ignoring the effects of it at the same time.

Sadly, my poor daughter went through middle school and high school being called names and being teased about her recurring Eczema flair ups and I had no clue. I was too busy being busy to notice.

One night after she had already graduated High School, I was cleaning the basement and I found a few of her old notebooks and I read page after page of songs and poetry; very sad and very angry memoirs. As I read though her journals I cried because my daughter had been suffering and I had no idea. I never helped her, at least I didn't think I had. I was beyond distraught with guilt and pain, but I thank God for Jesus! We had taught our daughter how to pray. We taught her to have a personal relationship with Jesus Christ. She had heard me pray. She had watched me cry and pray until things got better and that is how she made it through her storms.

I was going up to talk to her, with notebooks in hand and as I got closer to her bedroom, I heard her singing, I stood by her door. "In your eyes I am beautiful, pure and wonderful. No one's created like me. In your eyes I am priceless, royal and faultless, no heart's designed just like mine; for I am fearfully and wonderfully made, in your eyes I'm not the same, for I am fearfully and wonderfully made …" were the words I heard from a voice unlike any other. My baby girl had hurdled every storm and survived knowing that she was not what they said about her! She had redirected and saw herself from God's perspective, in essence, through his eyes and she knew that she was beautiful!

So, in case you failed at redirecting like I did. Perhaps you just couldn't put yourself in another

REDIRECTION

person's place. Perhaps you were too blinded by your own perception to possibly see things from another person's perception, try praying for the person you cannot understand. Try praying for yourself, ask God to open your eyes to another perspective. Ask God for discernment! Do whatever you have to do to change the intended outcome. No damage is too great, as a matter of fact, prayer prevents damage!

This subject goes beyond spouses and children. This is what we call, *immediate* family but we face similar challenges with our siblings, cousins, aunts and uncles. One by one, we must place ourselves in their places and pray for wisdom to see things from their perspectives. If their perceptions have become misguided by misunderstandings, rumors or past hurt it will have to be you to initiate the dialogue that restores any lost love. Why you? Because you are the one reading this book! God works in mysterious ways.

Let's go! Chin up. Make the call, send the text, initiate the dialogue with better outcomes in your mind. Remember, if you do what you've always done, you will get what you've always gotten. I cannot give you a script, but it sounds a little something like this. "My dear sister. I know there is something wrong with our relationship and It's probably my fault. I really want to resolve this and have a better relationship with you. Don't worry. I can take it. I have thick skin and I'm ready to hear whatever I need to hear to get this resolved. Tell me what the problem is." You will open up a dialogue for their story their way. A story from their perspective. This time listen carefully and do not be distracted by your own pride or your own defense. After hearing her painful truth, as misguided as it may seem; respect it as her truth. The very next words from you should start with, "I am so sorry …" If you're not quite ready for that yet, keep reading! There is much more.

REDIRECTION

THE ME NOBODY KNOWS

For some, relationship with others is not a challenge. We get along well with our families; we get along well with our co-workers and friends. We have learned to let people live and mind our own business about their affairs. We have learned how to have peace in our homes. We have learned to navigate around eggshells and not disturb the peace and to everyone on the outside of us, our life is the one to envy, but... Yes! There is always a "but". I must speak to the person who is having an inner-peace challenge.

Without doubt, most external problems stem from inner-peace problems. When people are not at peace within themselves, they often have a tendency to lash out at others. These outbursts are usually out of character for the individual and seem to come from nowhere. The person who has mastered external relationships is a delight to be around until they are faced with an inner-peace struggle that catches them off guard.

Cynthia McInnis

I cannot over-emphasize the importance of having complete inner-peace. The entire world is searching for it. When a person's mind is not at peace, nothing in his world works properly regardless to the superfluous accomplishments he attains in life and the mass accumulation of wealth he acquires. Ask any rich, famous, prosperous, accomplished drug-addict! How does someone as accomplished as Robin Williams commit suicide? How do people as uniquely gifted and talented as Whitney Houston, Elvis Presley and Michael Jackson, along with countless others, have the final stories that they had? Even, world renown religious leaders have been found wanting; suicide, drug addiction, alcoholism and depression do not escape them.

Admittedly, when I attempted to do a specific study on the quest for inner peace, I was bombarded with one philosophy after another, more than a million quotes by various world leaders and religious preceptors along with a plethora of suggestions, ideas and instructions. I thought, with all of this helpful information on how to

REDIRECTION

attain inner-peace, how is it that the suicide rate is still on the rise? How is it that suicide continues to plummet amongst the rich and famous? Why is the divorce rate sky-rocketing? I wish I had an answer that could possibly satisfy everyone and be the fix-all for all of the questions I just posed. Just as all of that information is only as helpful as it is accessed, my resolve would only be good to those who have accessed this book. So, I will continue prayerfully with this writing as if personalized just for you and not a ministry to the masses.

Attaining and maintaining inner-peace from day to day and relationship to relationship has many roads that lead to its success, however, this book focuses on redirection; changing perceptions for successful outcomes.

I can recall too many major incitements levied by the following five words, "What is really bothering you?" The keyword here is, *"really."* To ask a person what is bothering them almost never incites a riot. If they don't want you to know, or if they don't really know themselves, they will quickly answer, "nothing", and that will be it. When you add the word, *really* you have concluded that this level of outburst does not match the problem they have claimed. With that, you have initiated an unauthorized, unqualified psycho-therapy session or laymen's-level pastoral evaluation and the person is simply not having that. "Who in the world do you think you are to analyze me?" is what comes next and what may have been an attempt to resolve a heated situation had become an entirely different situation. Can anyone relate?

Trying to understand another's emotion is not trying to analyze the person. Putting yourself in their place is never trying to *find out what's really wrong with them.* It is more of trying to see what they see from their perception and once you are able to see it from their perception you may understand why they responded to the degree that they did. For example, a tantrum over one dirty dish left in the sink seems to be a bit much until you find out that dirty dishes left in the sink had been a serious issue time and time again in the past. While it still may not merit such a discourse, it is at least understanding their emotion. It is showing empathy.

REDIRECTION

Empathy is not trying to fix the problem, rather, it is understanding and entering into another's feelings.

When a situation has been exacerbated and everything is haywire and out of control anything other than empathy will only make the situation worse. We must get to the *why* before we attempt the *what* or the *how?* Questions like *What do you want me to do?* and *How can we resolve this?* Are questions that can only be answered after we get the truest, *why?*. That will start with empathy.

Empathy does not start with a wrong or right, a good or bad or any type of judgment. That is why redirection is not such an easy thing to attain. It is so easy to pass judgment. We do it to our children, we do it to our friends and we most definitely do it to ourselves. Very often, if we just leave a person to their own thoughts before responding to an adverse action, they'll *come to themselves* or *get themselves together*; at which point, it will be much easier to talk to them. They will, in essence, find *peace* within themselves and be able to communicate their feelings more rationally. It is this finding of peace, within ourselves, that becomes so important to conflict resolution. When we are able to redirect our own thoughts, change perceptions about our own situations and find peace, then, we will be better able to do that externally. In conversational language, this would be, *get yourself together before you try to get someone else together.*

The Scripture says, in Matthew 7:12, *"Therefore all things whatsoever ye would that men should do to you, do ye even so to them: for this is the law and the prophets."* We must first understand how to resolve internal conflicts before making attempts to resolve external conflicts in relationships. Sometimes I find myself arguing with myself about things. If I had left home without something very important, like, going on a bank-run to make a deposit and forgetting the money. Duhhhhh … I would call myself all kinds of crazy, stupid and retarded! Then I resolve that I'm simply doing too much at one time and I need to slow down and relax. In the moment, the negative adjectives best described me to myself but after redirecting my perception to a more reasonable one, one that made a lot more sense, I found peace. Now, if we could just do that

REDIRECTION

for others, we would be well on our way to better outcomes.

Later on. After I have made the bank deposit and I am at internal peace with myself, I should take the time to find out why my second response was not my first response. Why did I automatically go to the negative on myself? Is that what I do to others? More than likely, the answer is, "yes." If not and I am quick to give others the benefit of the doubt and go positive on their negatives, why can't I do that for myself? I really believe that what you do to yourself, you usually do to others, but a backward solution is to practice strong resolves for others and then try to make them work for yourself. Too many of us live far too externally and not nearly enough internally. By this, I mean we are very concerned about what people think of us. We have much too much to prove and we have too many self-serving agendas. We will give others the benefit of the doubt verbally while in our hearts we are simply trying to impress them. We want them to think we are so full of wisdom and empathy that they can trust us. This is only beneficial if it is truth! If we have not mastered redirection internally, it only takes one bout of emotional frustration with ourselves that leads to a lashing out, or seemingly ridiculous outburst to show these people that we are not really that wise or empathetic and we are not fit to trust.

This book proposes a season of introspection; getting to know, *the me nobody knows*. People will never truly know you if you do not truly know yourself. This includes, the good, the bad and the ugly. Knowing the good about ourselves is both necessary and detrimental. It is necessary if you are prone to self-hatred, low self-esteem or depression. It is detrimental if that is all you focus on and think that the *good one* is the only one.

By nature, we love ourselves; as self-hatred is considered some form of psychological dysfunction. However, most often, we find out what may be considered *bad or ugly* about ourselves from other people. Allow me to eliminate the information passed to us third or fourth hand. Hearing gossip passed from one person to another person to another person and finally to you is not the barometer you want to use to do a real examination of yourself. A real examination is considerable when some negative information about you

REDIRECTION

is coming from someone who loves you. People who love you will eventually tell you the truth. Remember, that is their truth. It is what they perceive as truth about you. The best way to handle it is to redirect. We must objectively hear what they are saying, dismissing judgment and resisting self-defense. Just hear it. If you can get past that point, pat yourself on the back. Sleep on it. Try to see what this person sees in you. See if it has any remote truth. If there is the slightest hint of truth, let that become your project. Your objective would now be to make certain that the hint of truth disappears forever. You do not need to prove anything to anyone, you need only to become a better person. What if there seems to be so much to fix? Remember your *why!* You are not trying to prove or impress anyone so give yourself as much time as you need to work on each thing at a time and you will find that working on you is a lifetime project. Love yourself for every change you make.

Do not be afraid to face the monsters. Preparing yourself for the cold, hard truth makes handling the lies a lot easier. It almost becomes funny because some of the lies people tell about you pale in comparison the hidden truth. The *Me they Know* is a saint compared to the *Me Nobody Knows* ... only they don't know it.

REDIRECTION

INTRODUCE YOURSELF

With each new year we are all tempted to herald the adage, *New Year, New Me!* With all of its cracks and crevices, challenges and doubts, it remains a good incentive. I believe it is noble for everyone to try to add to themselves as often as possible and why not at the beginning of a brand new year? Making New Year's resolutions are often criticized because, while the intentions are good, we often fail at keeping them. The spirit is willing, but the flesh is weak.

Perhaps our goals are simply unrealistic, and with a little insight and definition, a little *redirection,* we might be able to tailor them or scale them to fit our realistic abilities. Perhaps, we want the end results but are unwilling or unable to do the work required to get there. Redirection will help us to set the right goals to get our desired results.

One of the main goals for the new year is better health and/or better bodies. The dreaded New Year's Diet! We all know of the roller-coaster weight-loss plans. We have all spent money we really did not have, believing in a product we truly did not believe in. We all know there is no miracle, fat-burning, carbohydrate blocking juice, tea or pill. We have all said, *I'm only gonna use this for 2 weeks just to get the initial weight off and then to the gym I go!* We have all signed up for gym memberships that we just won't cancel because we really, really intend to go back ... one day.

Don't get nervous, I am not the one to slam-dunk anyone's roller-coaster ride, especially since I've been right in the seat behind you. The question, however, is why? Why do we keep doing what we keep doing and getting the same results? I believe that part of it is our insatiable desire to *do something*. We are not the type to quit or simply lay down in the battle and just let life happen to us. Somewhere inside of us, we are saying we will not die from the same diseases that killed our loved ones. We will not just sit there and take it and let life handle us! Something is better than nothing.

We'll get up early a few days or a few weeks even, put on our sneakers and sweats and without combing a hair, brushing a tooth or having a piece of

REDIRECTION

toast, dash right out there onto the pavement or that treadmill at the gym and *do something.* We feel so good about ourselves that we keep those stinky sweats on until someone shows up that we can tell! *Yeah, I just came back from my workout!* If no one shows up, we pose, with face sweat gleaming, snap that selfie and post it to every social media platform we can. Why? We want to hear somebody say, "Go Girl!" "Keep up the good work!" or "I should have been out there with you."

In this case, we learn something new about ourselves. Not only do we desire better health and/or better bodies, we also desire applause, validation and support. If you are shaking your head *no* and saying I don't need anyone's validation, ask yourself why you just got on the defense. Someone has spread a rumor that wanting applause, validation and support is a bad thing. Well it's not! It is the nature of human beings to want to be *seen.*

When a baby cries, he's seeking someone's attention. When the child finally poops in the potty, he seeks some type of applause. We have graduation ceremonies, birthday parties and anniversary galas for the very same reasons. We desire applause, validation and support. We all want it and we all need it. This is the reason we do more when we are competing than we do on our own. A good healthy weight-loss challenge does two things; it helps us to reach our goals and gets us the applause we need to keep moving.

That marathon runner keeps going when he sees and hears the applause of the sideline and the voice of his supporters. This is absolutely respectable! When we have a partner on the journey, we can encourage each other not to quit. This is when choosing the right partner becomes major. Healthy, honest competition is an incentive but competition that comes from a selfish agenda will always cause a change of motive. My partner has to be someone who is willing to help me when I am weak, not compare my challenges to his. If I get tired sooner, he will slow down to help me, not call me lazy or make me feel bad. If he cannot walk as fast as I can, I will slow down until my partner is able to pick up his pace. I need to understand that we are not in a race to win but a marathon and our goal is to make it to the finish line, whenever, together.

REDIRECTION

A partner is not a coach. The coach will push and encourage me to do more than I think I am able to do; a partner stays with me until I can. This book encourages forming and mending relationships; developing partnerships that help us to achieve our goals and foster better outcomes in life. The main person in the partnership is *me*. I have to be the partner I need ... I need to introduce the *old me* to the *new me!*

I must get to know her from every valid perception. I must see her through an often painful lens called *the whole truth*. I must answer every *why* that I can before I try to sell her to anyone else. Why does she start things and not finish? Why does she work so hard? Why does she keep making changes? Why doesn't she have many friends? Why do people shy away from her? Why are people so drawn to her? Why is she not trusted? Why do people tend to share their personal business with her? Why does she feel like a victim? This list of questions can go on forever, but she must remember that every answer is for *her*. She must endeavor to answer with all truth because change cannot happen without truth. *Behold, thou desirest truth in the inward parts; and in the hidden part thou shalt make me to know wisdom.* Psalms 51:6

I had an experience many years ago that may help someone. I served in church with another sister whom I really loved dearly. I didn't know much about her personally, she came from where she came from and I came from where I came from but we both shared an obvious love for the church and the work of the church. We had both become front-line soldiers in the church and were responsible for much of what happened there. I thought she was a great blessing to the church because she was relentless in her desire to do whatever she could to help.

It appeared to me that while I thought the world of her, she didn't care much for me. I learned later why that was kind of common, but It was really starting to get to me. One day I was sitting between her and another sister and she was reaching over me to tap the other sister to comment on common things like, a person's nice shoes or handbag. These were things she surely could have shared with me but she chose not to. She

REDIRECTION

knew the other sister the same way she knew me, through the church. It was annoying but more than that it was very hurtful. I had my history of bad days but none with her. I immediately started to think like a victim. The other people who had problems with me must have been talking to her about me. There was no possible way that she could have come up with a bad feeling about me, after all, I liked her.

After that I just decided to avoid her and put her in the category with the rest of my *haters.* The problem with that was that I had an idea of why the others didn't care for me. I was not very nice to them for whatever reasons; but I had no problems with this sister, and I wanted to know why. Everything in me said, *So what! It's her loss! Blah, blah, blah* but something else in me wanted to fix that. I could not sleep. I just couldn't keep seeing her in every service, worshipping and working in church with her, knowing I had obviously done something to her that she did not like.

One day, while I was at work, I picked up the phone and called her. I had already prepared myself for whatever she had to say. I talked to myself and told myself that this would not end in an argument or a fight. When she answered we did the regular church niceties and then I went to work. I told her I was calling because we work together, and we worship in the same church and it was obvious to me that I had done something to cause her to dislike me and I wanted her to feel free and comfortable to tell me what I had done. At first, she said there was nothing wrong and she had no problems with me, but I knew better and so did she. I worked hard to assure her that I could handle it and my only reason for the call was to try to resolve that problem whatever it was. She needed to trust me enough to know that I was not starting trouble and did not want to fight. I refused to let her get off the phone without making that crystal clear. It would be either she had no reason for real and it was just some form of jealousy or she had a reason that she was uncomfortable sharing with me.

    I would not go to another person and try to find out. That would have caused more problems. I wanted to hear it from her. You might say I was a glutton for punishment but churchwork and worship meant too much to me to be tainted by something that could be

REDIRECTION

resolved. The Bible says, "*Moreover if thy brother shall trespass against thee, go and tell him his fault between thee and him alone: if he shall hear thee, thou has gained a brother.*" Matthew 18:15 I really believe that is the way God intended, even though it is popular for one to go and tell the pastor or some other person, I believe that certain matters can be resolved privately and permanently.

I was finally able to gain her trust and she began to tell me what the problem was. It turned out that I was doing something that I always did, thinking it was harmless and playful sarcasm, but it was affecting her greatly. I honestly had no idea that she had heard me or that it would be offensive to her. I never intended to make her feel the way *my actions* made her feel. I was very sorry. I would never do that again. I apologized and immediately I felt a release of freedom between us. Then the unexpected happened, she then asked me if she had done anything to me that made me feel uncomfortable. I began to say this and that and the conversation ended pleasantly and with much relief. The two of us worked harmoniously in ministry, worshipped together, laughed and loved and remain great friends to this day.

I had to put myself in her shoes, hear her truth and admit where I was wrong and guess what, I didn't die! In fact, it brought life and liberty to an otherwise destroyed relationship and season of fake or painful worship that would have been mixed with emotional ups and downs.

That girl in the introduction had to be better! She was determined to be a better person, a better Christian and a better friend. And then she got married ... and she had to introduce that girl to the married version of herself. The married one is, so far, a 27-year work in progress. Please keep her in prayer but I think she's going to make it!

REDIRECTION

THE ENEMIES AROUND US

At some point we must desire more. We must endeavor to live our best lives and our lives must match the desires that almighty God has for us. I do not believe that the best life is the life that does not have enemies, but the life that can identify and understand the purpose of every enemy. Every enemy has a purpose whether it be an enemy within or without. The English word *enemy* is derived from the Latin word, *inimicus, unfriendly or inimical, hostile* and is defined as an opposing military force. It is clear that an enemy's initial purpose is never good.

All enemies come with a purpose to do harm and therefore must be met with opposition and force. Once it is determined to be an enemy, we must fight tooth and nail to destroy its fulfillment in our lives. So now, let us see unhealthy eating habits and lifestyles as enemies, let's see unhealthy relationships as enemies, let's see painful hurt as an enemy and go after these enemies like a mother for her child! A father for his family! A God for his creation!

We must desire to be made whole; nothing missing and nothing broken in our lives. If our natural family relationship is falling apart it is an enemy that must be defeated. If our marriage is at its wit's end, we absolutely must not give it up to an enemy! If we can't get along with our church family, that is an enemy at work. Enemies must be defeated. *He saith unto them, an enemy hath done this* ... Matthew 13:28a

The last time I checked, we had power over all enemies! *"Behold, I give you power to tread on serpents and scorpions, and over all the power of the enemy: and nothing shall by any means hurt you."* Luke 10:19. I promised you that I would not preach to you in this book, but this verse right here will preach! Once we see these detrimental relationships as enemies, we will begin to stomp on them and eventually stomp them out.

If it means we have to re-visit the past painful divorces, baby-mama, baby-daddy breakups, friendship fall-outs one by one and take ownership of our parts, for real, then so be it. Holding on to pain is self-destructive.

REDIRECTION

Holding on to blame is equally self-destructive. These things send messages through the bloodline, spoken or unspoken. Unforgiveness and pain have aromas. You can't see it but it gets on your clothes and fills up every crevice of your home. It gets on your sheets and causes nightmares. It gets in your children's pajamas and they're sleeping with enemies they cannot see. They wake up with hatred for people they never had a problem with. An enemy has done this!

How long will we remain defeated by things we can fix? I didn't say people, because we are not in the business of fixing people, that's God's job. We can fix many of the problems caused by the things we, as people, have done. We can make these unsolved mysteries and unresolved disgruntlements a thing of the past.

Cynthia McInnis

FIGHT YOUR FIGHT!

Sometimes you have to choose to fight the fight, have the argument and bring things to the surface if you want it resolved. Buried serious emotions and feelings only come to surface with a greater force. I get it! Sometimes it is just easier to fake the funk. It is much less time-consuming to say you agree than to have to explain why you don't agree. You've tried that; only to find out that the person who asked for your opinion did not want your opinion, they wanted your approval of a decision they had already made. You fell for it the first time and perhaps the second time but by the third time, your opinion became whatever they wanted it to be, it was just easier. Weeks went by, then months and eventually years of being the *yes-man* became all too easy. You started having real conversations with yourself in your mind and that is where you expressed your real opinion.

REDIRECTION

The problem with this form of *silent peace* is that it does not end well. Eventually the silent partner will speak and the later in life that this person decides to break his or her silence, the more devastating the end results will be. It is then that both partners find out that it may have been better for them to have fought it out. Questions like, *Are you serious? Was I that bad? Are you making this up because you've found someone else? And finally, ... Why didn't you say anything?*

Now, it all comes out. *I've tried to say something but you ... every time I tried to tell you, you ...You were impossible. You were unfair. You were selfish.* The person on the other side of that *You! You! You!* is certainly not going to just sit there and take it. It is a lot to swallow, all at once, to be accused of being responsible for years of unhappiness in the life of someone you have loved and thought were reasonably happy. This will not end well without redirection.

The accused must inhale, exhale and try to put himself in the place of the accuser. This time he must not try to figure why the accuser is saying this and why he is saying it now; he must listen to what the accuser is saying as if it is something he had been holding back for years. The accused must use wisdom to validate the accusation as this person's truth, regardless to the length of time that has passed. Somehow or another he must put aside the questions of why it took so long to confront him and focus on the accusation as if it were a *right now* occurrence.

How hard is that? To some, impossible but after reading this book, it may become more possible than not. First, I want to speak to the wife who has quivered in the background, walked on eggshells trying desperately to avoid confrontation and now you are angry. You feel like you have lost yourself in the shadow of some monster's life. I hope you're sitting down. Inhale, exhale and try to answer some of these questions. Whose decision was it for you to stay silent about the serious issues in your life? Let's get this perfectly clear. I am not talking about choosing your battles to avoid unnecessary friction in your home. That is called wisdom. I am referring to the times that you were hurting legitimately. The times when you lay awake in the darkness with tears flowing from cheek to cheek. The times when you found

REDIRECTION

yourself burning, teeth grinding and holding back sound while he lay beside you in the darkness snoring to kingdom come absolutely oblivious to what was going on inside of you. How about the times when you had a real answer to a real question but left it alone because you thought it didn't matter to him anyway? These are the times for which I will ask you again, whose decision was it for you to keep silent? If you were afraid, whose decision was it for you to stay with someone you were so afraid of? Whose decision was it to wait, and wait and wait?

I already know the answers. The decisions were yours. Before you get offended, please know that these questions may sound intimidating, but they are not. They answer questions that may not have been asked, such as, who had the power to confront? Who had the strength to continue to live in silence all of this time? Who had to have redirected, regrouped and reconsidered over and over again to stay in the marriage all of these years and finally ... who has the power, the strength and the tenacity to fix this right now?

It's too late to go back to all of those times and get real answers. Who remembers every detail of every event? Perhaps you do but he certainly does not, remember, you never said it. Be kind, be tactful and be considerate, even if you feel you were never given those benefits. This book is about moving forward and getting better outcomes. If we think like we've always thought, we will get what we have always gotten. My dear sister, you must admit to yourself and to him that it was *your* mistake to keep silent and allow this pain to eat you up inside. You must admit that some of the anger you feel is your own. You punked out of a fight that you could not be sure would have even happened. You didn't learn to fight! I am not talking about physical confrontation. *"For the weapons of our warfare are not carnal, but mighty through God to the pulling down of strong holds."* 2 Corinthians 10:4

The good thing is, it's never too late to learn to fight your fight. It starts with a reintroduction and walks its way through truth and necessity. This means you must deal in complete truth and only bother with things that are necessary for your relationship's survival. No

REDIRECTION

time for the trivial, we are at war here! Anything worth having is certainly worth fighting for, even if you don't feel like it at the moment. The instrument for weighing its value must be a spiritual one, not simply emotional. It has to be faith over facts and facts over feelings!

Very recently I was ear hustling an argument between my two sons. The older proclaimed his frustration with the younger's apparent lack of interest in the activities at a youth meeting at the church. He was livid about the younger's cell phone use and obvious disinterest during the discussion, facial and body language when confronted about it and overall lack of respect for him as a youth ministry leader. Well it was hot!

While I listened to the younger's adamant rejection of his brother's description of him, I could hear his anger and frustration welling up. "He cannot determine that I was not interested! He cannot tell how I was feeling! I was not on my phone the whole time! He has come to a wrong opinion about me!" It had gotten so hot that, by then, my husband had intervened.

I understood clearly why my husband would get involved. Lack of interest, disrespect and nonchalant attitudes are infectious and spread through the body like a disease, especially between brothers. No one wants to be in charge of a project and his own family members appear unsupportive. As my husband refereed the heated debate, what I heard next is the reason I decided to add this one of many arguments to this work.

My older son said, "Dad, I understand why he is so upset and why he is strongly defending himself. I understand because I used to do the same thing when you would tell me about my body language! While I am watching him, I am seeing myself. I didn't see what you saw at the time. Now that I am a leader, I can see from a leader's perspective and I understand it." He then turned to his younger brother and said, "You have to try to see yourself from my perspective in order to understand this. Until you do that, you will continue to be on the defensive."

Well, the way my antennae went up at that point was invigorating! It appeared that my son had already read this book. He had gotten it! Eureka! This was

REDIRECTION

exactly the point. Both of them were right when seeing from their own perspectives but when time and maturity came together for one, he was able to see that a change of perception was necessary for better outcomes. He was ultimately saying, *see this from where I am sitting*. The younger son must see himself as a leader and wonder how such body-language would appear to him. He must factor in other added leadership frustrations such as lateness, absenteeism and lack of participation from others in the group and then see how much more frustrating it is when this behavior is coming from his own brother, who he thinks, if anyone would be trying to help, it would be his own family members.

I cannot tell you that the younger brother was able to grasp the entire moment, change his perception and understand it clearly from his brother's eyes, but I will tell you that the older son's confession of misdirected perception in the past was very impactful. It reconfirmed my repetition of a quote from Bishop James R. Chambers of St. Mary's church, that "Time is the great revealer!" We cannot afford to let time become the enemy of our faith. For some reading this book, You may have to use time as your ally and faith as your momentum to wait until someone has had his own experience and/or have matured enough to see from your perception and perspective. You may even have to give yourself time to see from another person's perception in order to forgive and move forward.

Whether or not to forgive a person is a no-brainer for me. Jesus says in Mark 11:26 *"But if you do not forgive, neither will your Father which is in heaven forgive your trespasses."* We tend to base our willingness to forgive on the severity of the violation but that is not how forgiveness works. If God has forgiven you for anything you should also forgive others for anything. This is a very strong concept and makes justifying divorce difficult. The truth is forgiving is not forgetting. For this reason, divorce, separations and break-ups continue and are on the incline. As long as I keep remembering the violation, I am challenged to leave the relationship.

Let's see how God handles this. Isaiah 43:25 *"I, even I, am he that blotteth out thy transgressions for mine own sake, and will not remember thy sins."* God

REDIRECTION

blots out and *will* not remember. It does not say he *cannot* remember it says he *will* not remember. It is his will not to remember our sins and therefore frees him up to keep loving us *past our sins*.

If a person is willing to try to change his or her perception about something that is instrumental in the devastation of a relationship it is like repenting. Asking for forgiveness is getting a pass, but repenting is changing the mind about what was done and re-evaluating those factors that caused them to do it in the first place. It is changing perceptions for a better outcome. It is not easy but it is doable and time may prove that it was well worth it.

THE WHY?

I have been challenged often with questions about forgiveness. Some of the most devastating and heart-wrenching circumstances have been presented to me for counselling. Many times, I had been taken aback by the callous actions of people who say they love each other and then asked, *how am I supposed to forgive this person?* Each time I have been forced by conviction to ask, "Why do you think this person is behaving or has behaved this way?" I get it! Even I didn't care why in some cases. I was just as prone as the *victim* to skip the *why* and get to the *what to do,* but the *why* is what can at least start the redirection process.

Understanding a person's, *why* has to come from the person, not from your own perception. I have shared with you how often people can believe the worst about themselves and give other people a *why*. The rape victim who believes she is the cause of her assault, the child who believes he is the cause of his parent's divorce or the abused wife who believes she is the cause of her

REDIRECTION

abuse are examples of why we cannot be the ones to answer another person's *why*.

Simply asking a person why is usually not going to get the matter resolved. For many, they have not the slightest clue why they behave the way they do. For others, they will never admit that part of the problem is theirs or that the behavior is even a problem. I have heard abusers say things like, "If she would just shut-up she would not get hit." In essence, he is saying that the reason he violates, hurts, humiliates and/or abuses the person he loves is simply because *she* did not shut-up. He lost control and physically abused a lady who he loves because *she* did not shut-up. He got arrested and is sitting in a jail cell for domestic violence, all because *she* did not shut-up and he is O.K. with that! I think not. This man needs counseling to find his real *why*.

Sadly, it takes some people much too long to admit the need for help. Relationships are destroyed, families are devastated, children are traumatized, and life becomes a series of unsolved mysteries. This is why we need spiritual guidance, psychological therapy and peer-interaction. When life has finished with a man or a woman and caused them to admit that they have a problem they will seek their *whys*. It is my prayer that they have a good pastor who can direct them to help from the Scripture and offer sincere and honest prayer. While I do not discourage other forms of counseling and guidance, I prefer the more biblical and spiritual form.

When confronting *whys,* it is important to know that people are often seeing themselves from the victim perception. The victim who is victimizing will always give himself an out. He will always use his own victimization as an excuse. I read a very interesting article about the Victim Mentality on lonerwolf.com, that I will share with you here.

When we have a victim mentality, we filter our **entire existence** through a paranoid narrow mental lens that is used to perceive other people and reality. While it's important to claim the role of victim if we have genuinely been victimized or abused, *we cannot move on with our lives unless we step out of the victim role and into the survivor role.*

REDIRECTION

What is a Victim Mentality?

Victim mentality is a psychological term that refers to a type of dysfunctional mindset which seeks to feel persecuted in order to gain attention or avoid self-responsibility. **People who struggle with the victim mentality are convinced that life is not only beyond their control but is out to deliberately hurt them.** This belief results in constant blame, finger-pointing, and pity parties that are fueled by pessimism, fear, and anger. Simply put, having a victim mentality means that you blame other people and circumstances for the unhappiness you feel.

How Self-Victimization Develops

No one is born with a victim mentality, just as no one is born clinically depressed or anxious. Instead, the victim mentality is an acquired personality trait, meaning that it is the result of early life conditioning and coping mechanisms. Most victims were victimized in some way as children, whether that was through physical abuse, sexual abuse, emotional abuse or psychological abuse. Self-victimization can also develop through the codependent relationships we had with our parents, or simply by observing and adopting the unhealthy victim mentality exhibited by one or more of our family members. However, although what happens to us as children is completely beyond our control, it is our responsibility as adults to step into our power and reclaim responsibility for our happiness.

9 Benefits of Being a Victim

Playing the victim actually has a number of juicy perks. These rewards make it very difficult to break out of such a mindset, which is why most victims seem to be so emotionally invested in perpetuating this type of toxic behavior.

Some of the perks include the following:
- Not having to take responsibility for anything
- Other people lavishing you with attention
- Other people feeling sorry for you
- Other people are less likely to criticize or upset you
- You have the "right" to complain
- You're more likely to get what you want

REDIRECTION

- You feel interesting because you get to tell people all of your stories
- You don't have to feel bored because there's too much drama going on
- You get to avoid and bypass anger because you're too busy feeling sad
-

Can you see some underlying patterns starting to emerge here?

Playing the victim actually gives you a lot of power: power to avoid responsibility, power to feel "righteously" sad and persecuted, power to avoid uncomfortable emotions, and power to manipulate other people.

The Dark Side of Playing the Victim

The majority of people who play the victim do so unconsciously, or unintentionally. Even so, the victim role does involve a tremendous amount of manipulation and string-pulling. People in relationships or friendships with victims often report feeling like puppets who mold into whatever the victim believes they are or wants them to be.

Having other people feel sorry for you is an easy way to wrap them around your little finger. This unconscious craving to control others through their sympathies is really only a way for the mind to reinforce its belief in the "I'm a victim" ego identity.

There is a lot of comfort and artificial "safety" in playing the victim identity. Not only does it reward you with not having to take responsibility for any of your behavior (because "other people" are always responsible), but it also prevents you from feeling uncomfortable emotions like guilt and anger, while at the same time making you feel "cared for" by others.

Playing the victim is also often used by abusive and/or sociopathic people who use this role to keep a tight emotional leash on those close to them. For example, a narcissistic person might constantly put down their partner, then fixate on the one time their partner snapped and called them a "monster," making it seem like they are in fact the "abused one." Or a physically abusive person might use the excuse that they "always have to put up with the other person" as a reason for beating up their partner.

As we can see, **the "poor me" attitude can be used on both sides of the human spectrum: both seemingly "normal" people and more extreme and dysfunctional psychopathic people.** For example, in codependent relationships, self-victimization can be used by the enabler and the abuser, and sometimes both at the same time in a kind of power struggle.

There is no one "type" of person that fits into the victim role, so it's wrong to say that only narcissists or sociopaths adopt this role. I have personally seen all types of people play this role: from sweet old grandmothers to teenagers, mothers, fathers, professionals, and even "spiritually awakened" people.

23 Signs of the Victim Mentality
Are you, or is someone you love, playing the victim? Here are some common signs to look out for:
- You're constantly blaming other people or situations for feeling miserable
- You possess a "life is against me" philosophy

- You're cynical or pessimistic
- You see your problems as catastrophes and blow them out of proportion
- You think others are purposely trying to hurt you
- You believe you're the only one being targeted for mistreatment
- You keep reliving past painful memories that made you feel like a victim
- Even when things go right, you find something to complain about
- You refuse to consider other perspectives when talking about your problems
- You feel powerless and unable to cope effectively with a problem or life in general
- You feel attacked when you're given constructive criticism
- You believe you're not responsible for what happens in your life (others are)
- You believe that everyone is "better off" than you
- You seem to enjoy feeling sorry for yourself

REDIRECTION

- You attract people like you (who complain, blame, and feel victimized by life)
- You believe that the world is a scary, mostly bad, place
- You enjoy sharing your tragic stories with other people
- You have a habit of blaming, attacking, and accusing those you love for how you feel
- You feel powerless to change your circumstances
- You expect to gain sympathy from others, and when you don't get it, you feel upset
- You refuse to analyze yourself or improve your life
- You tend to "one-up" people when it comes to sharing traumatic experiences
- You're constantly putting yourself down

As we can see, the permanent sense of being a victim is deeply destructive both internally, and externally.

How to Stop Being a Victim
If you're reading this article because you suspect that you might be clinging to a victim mentality, here are some tips that can help you step out of this toxic role:

1. Start replacing "you" with "I"
For example, instead of saying "you make me feel so angry," you can replace that statement with, "I feel so angry when I hear you say that." This simple trick can help you learn to take more self-responsibility for your happiness.

2. See yourself as a survivor
      A victim argues with life, a survivor embraces it. A victim dwells in the past, a survivor lives in the present. A victim believes they're helpless, a survivor takes back control over their life. Although the victim mentality is addictive, the survivor mentality is much more empowering in the long term. Once you start seeing yourself as a survivor, you'll begin to feel better about life and you'll attract other people for the right reasons. Listening to a survivor is much more refreshing

REDIRECTION

and inspiring than listening to a victim wallow in self-pity.

3. Be kind and compassionate towards yourself

In other words, be careful about becoming a victim of being a victim! This role isn't something you choose: you developed it as a result of childhood conditioning. Be gentle with yourself and practice self-love. Explore your core wounds and core beliefs that compound your victim identity and replace self-loathing with self-compassion. If you're struggling to get past the victim role, practice self-care by seeing a therapist. Experiment with practices such as journaling, affirmations, NLP (http://www.nlpu.com/NewDesign/NLPU_WhatIsNLP.html) CBT, and other forms of self-love.

4. Explore your mistaken beliefs

Mistaken beliefs create anxiety, depression, anger, and blame. We explore the twelve different types of mental traps here (https://lonerwolf.com/anxiety-and-depression/). You will probably be stunned by how many types of mistaken beliefs you have unknowingly adopted!

5. Ask "What thought is creating this suffering?"

All suffering originates in beliefs that go unquestioned and unexamined in our minds. When we attach to these thoughts, we suffer. Remember that you don't need to believe the thoughts in your head: thoughts are simply fluctuations of energy that we assign meaning to. Practicing meditation can help you notice how transient thoughts are.

6. Practice being thankful

Gratitude is a simple but powerful way to remind yourself that life is not as miserable as you perceive it to be. Each day, try to find ten things that you're thankful for. You might like to keep a gratitude journal in which you write these ten things down, or simply name them mentally. Try to feel sincerely thankful for having these things.

REDIRECTION

7. Affirm self-responsibility

Start to notice all the ways you bypass self-responsibility. Be ruthlessly honest and examine how gaining sympathy from others makes you feel special and continues the cycle of pointing the finger at others. You might like to use an affirmation such as "I am responsible for my life" or "I am empowered to create change" to help you reprogram this unconscious need to play the victim. You might also like to do something that builds your confidence and actually shows you that you're capable … or reflect on something in the past that you overcame successfully.

8. Perform an act of kindness for another

When we play the victim, we tend to be solely focused on ourselves. Get yourself out of your head by doing something nice for another person you love. Realizing that you can feel good without manipulating another person is an important way to cut the addiction the self-victimization.

The article goes further to describe the Victim Complex. You can read the entire article at https://lonerwolf.com/victim-mentality/. While I am admittedly not an expert on such psychological subjects, I can say that the article was a great help to me, so much so that I have shared it with you.

REDIRECTION

THE BUSINESS

Part of who I am is what I read. As an avid reader, I have come across some astonishing and helpful information from some who have since become my favorite authors. When you have read something that is so impactful that you tend to repeat it often, you also want to refer to it in your own books. I could simply re-tell this story but I have decided to include it so you can read it for yourself. The writer to which I refer is Rabbi Daniel Lapin from his book, Business Secrets of the Bible. While the entire book is mind-altering and intriguing, for this work, I refer to the below passage.

We have already established that anyone who works is technically in business, whether they are a bus driver or barista, coffee shop owner or CEO. Secretaries should, even as hourly employees, consider themselves in business. Because they are. They are in the business of providing secretarial services, even if at that moment, they might only have one customer, their employer. This is not a matter of semantics, but an important distinction that requires you to change the way you think. The company that writes your paycheck every two weeks is not your employer; they are your customer. Adopt this mind-set and everything changes. You are free from the daily grind— free to grow your business and serve your customers, your fellow man.

One time, while visiting a church in Dallas, I imparted this lesson to a thoughtful audience. Afterward, a woman, a single mother who worked as a checker at a supermarket, came up to me and told me she was trying to apply this biblical business secret to her life. "I work very hard, but I just am having a hard time wrapping my head around it." She said that she always thought of the people in line as her customers. How could her employer be a customer too, she wanted to know. I invited her to the hotel where I was staying to have a cup of coffee with my wife and me so that we could discuss this principle in detail. What it boils down to is this: People feel an obligation to their customers that they do not feel to their employer. So often we forget that our employer is our customer. Remember, everyone is in business, even if their one and only customer is their boss.

REDIRECTION

Successful employees treat and value their bosses the same way successful shopkeepers treat the people who patronize their establishments. One feels a sense of ownership over and obligation toward their customers. When you realize that your boss is really your customer, you will have an easier time treating him or her with due deference.

A good analogy is the difference in the way we treat rental cars and our own cars. You never take a rental car to a car wash. You take it back dirty. What do you care? It doesn't belong to you! I am not saying this is the way we should think, but it is the way we do think. It is the same way with work. When things are busy at your job and your employer needs help, many people just want to go home and let someone else worry about it. But if you owned the shop at which you worked, you would never treat a customer this way. Imagine I am trying to build a small business, say, as a roofer, and I am about to go home for the day and the phone rings— it is a potential customer. He says, "Hey, Lapin, you're a roofer, right? I met you at Synagogue the other day and I heard somebody say you were in roofing." He tells me his roof just started leaking through the ceiling and he is scared of damage. If he's my customer, how do I react? I say I will be there right away and drop everything because somebody needs me. It is not just doctors who do that, but all successful business professionals. Everybody in business does and should. Some people may thinly veil their own laziness or misplaced priorities by dressing them up in misplaced morals. They may say that the business professional should seek you putting the needs of another human being before your own personal wants. Life requires this kind of balancing act of your personal and professional lives, and you do not want your kids seeing you putting your personal self before your professional self. We want our children to be happy, yes, but first and foremost we want to instill in them proper values.

    There are times when you put your own wants aside for the sake of a customer precisely because doing so is in the best interests of your child, both financially and morally. You want to teach your kids the importance of taking responsibility for and ownership of their customers. This is what I explained to the single mother

REDIRECTION

in Dallas when we were having coffee at my hotel. And slowly she began to understand. She began to see that the people in her line were not just customers, they were the customers of her customer— her employer. "And I have to take care of all the customers of my customers," she said, "because that is my job and my duty to my main customer, who is my employer." I told her I couldn't have said that better myself. It may interest you to know what became of her. This realization completely changed because regulars wanted to say hello to her as they checked out. One day a person came in whom she had never seen before and asked when she got off work. At first, she thought he was hitting on her and she spurned the advance. "You misunderstand me," he said. "I don't want to date you. I want to hire you." He gave her a business card from his real estate company. She didn't understand but agreed to meet later at a local coffee shop. There he offered her a job. He needed someone to work the front desk and serve as the face of first contact with potential clients. He had been watching how she treated people in the checkout line and decided she was perfect for the job. He offered her a salary and benefits that far surpassed the minimum wage she was making as a checker. This has completely turned around both her life and the life of the child she supports. And how did she accomplish this? By chasing wealth? No, not exactly, though she seized upon an opportunity at hand. But that opportunity was only at hand because she first put in the effort to communicate and collaborate effectively with the customers already around her. *Lapin, Daniel. Business Secrets from the Bible: Spiritual Success Strategies for Financial Abundance (p. 58). Wiley. Kindle Edition.*

I will say to you that the story of the supermarket checker is one that inspired me to write this book. When she began to see herself differently, her story changed. Her life took on *redirection.* By changing her perception, she obtained a much better outcome. I wrote this book for those who yearn better outcomes and are willing to do whatever it takes to get them. I wrote it for those persons who are sick and tired of being sick and tired and really want to see change. I wrote it for those who are in a seemingly never-ending revolving door of the mundane and more of the same. I wrote it for those who

REDIRECTION

have reached a glass ceiling, ice on the surface and a dead-end street at life. I want you to know that you have the power to change your outcomes and it begins with changing perceptions.

Haggai 2:3a says, *"Who is left among you that saw this house in her first glory? And how do you see it now?* The prophet was ready to effect change. After having rebuilt Solomon's temple, the prophet had to comfort the people that were grieved at the comparative poverty of the new temple. Many of the priests and Levites and chief fathers who had seen Solomon's temple wept with a loud voice. Solomon's temple was made with much more wealth and splendor and the new one was much less glamorous. He challenges their perceptions by asking the question, *how do you see it now?*

The prophet identifies the present with Solomon's temple, as being adapted for the same purposes, to fill the same place in the national life, built on the same hallowed spot, and partly with the same materials. In the Jews' eyes there was only one temple. They must change their perception about the temple and its true purpose. God assures them in verse number 7 that He would fill the house with His glory! Once the new temple is filled with the glory of God, the stones erecting it do not matter; whether it be solid gold of any other substance, it pales in comparison to the glory of God. Verse 9 says, *"The glory of this latter house shall be greater than the former, saith the Lord of hosts: and in this place will I give peace, saith the Lord of hosts.*

What was of true importance to the Jews was not how magnificently built the temple was but to have the glory of God present. The glory of God would bring them peace. How many of us are in a continuous state of contention? Too many of us are discontent with our relationships, our families, our homes, our jobs, our places of worship and even ourselves. We need peace. This book was written for you.

I trust that I have touched on enough areas to scratch the surface of redirection for you. It is not easy to do but it is very much doable, remember, you can do ALL things through Christ who strengthens you. All things, means all things.

www.ingramcontent.com/pod-product-compliance
Lightning Source LLC
LaVergne TN
LVHW041546070426
835507LV00011B/951